PEACE
OVER
BURDENS

PEACE OVER BURDENS

This book is a work of creative nonfiction based on real-life experiences. Names, locations, and certain identifying details may have been changed to protect privacy. Any resemblance to actual persons or events is not coincidental.

Scripture quotations, if used, are taken from the Holy Bible, unless otherwise noted.

ISBN: 979-8-34841-072-8

First Edition: March 2026

Cover design and interior layout by Khalilah H. Purnell
Printed in the United States of America

For speaking engagements, bulk orders, or media inquiries, please contact:
bookingkhalilahpurnell@gmail.com

Table of Contents

Part III: The Release

Part IV: Becoming

Part V: Peace

Author's Note

There comes a point when survival stops being enough. You realize you don't just want to make it through; you want to live without carrying everything that hurt you.

Peace is not the absence of struggle.
It is the decision to stop letting struggle define you.

For a long time, I confused strength with endurance. I thought being strong meant holding everything together, swallowing everything quietly, and proving I could survive no matter the cost. But strength without peace is just exhaustion with a title.

I learned that some burdens were never mine to carry.
Other people's expectations.
Other people's projections.
Other people's failures disguised as my responsibility.

Peace is choosing to put those things down without guilt.

Peace is understanding that closure is not always a conversation. Sometimes it is a boundary. Sometimes it is distance. Sometimes it is simply deciding that your heart deserves rest.

I no longer chase explanations.
I no longer beg for understanding.
I no longer shrink to make other people comfortable.

Peace taught me that I do not need to be loud to be powerful. I do not need to be perfect to be worthy. And I do not need permission to protect my spirit.

Peace is not selfish.
It is survival with wisdom.

I still feel.
I still care.
But I no longer bleed for people who would not hold me when I was broken.

Peace is choosing myself without apology.
Peace is releasing what I cannot change.
Peace is honoring who I am becoming.

And every day I remind myself:

I deserve peace more than I deserve to carry what was never meant to stay.

Dedication

This book is dedicated to every soul who has ever carried more than they were meant to bear.
To those who learned how to survive in silence, pray through confusion, and keep believing while their hearts were heavy.

To those who showed up for everyone else while quietly falling apart.
To those who kept trusting God even when the answers were delayed, unclear, or painful.
To those who chose healing instead of hardness, faith instead of fear, and peace instead of bitterness.

This is for the ones who learned that strength is not found in pretending,
but in surrender.
Not in endurance alone,
but in release.

May these pages remind you that your tears were seen,
your prayers were heard,
your waiting was not wasted,
and your healing matters.

You are not weak for feeling.
You are not forgotten in your struggle.
You are not behind in your journey.

You are becoming.

And this book is for you.

Introduction

Why Peace Had to Come First

You don't wake up one morning and suddenly decide that peace matters more than everything else. It usually happens after you've tried every other way to survive. After you've spent years being strong, patient, forgiving, understanding, and faithful, even when it was costing you more than you wanted to admit.

For a long time, you convince yourself that carrying heavy things is just part of life. You tell yourself that being tired means you're doing something right. That being overwhelmed means you're responsible, and That being quiet means you're mature. So, you keep going, even when your body is tired, your mind is full, and your spirit feels stretched thin.

You learn how to show up for other people while ignoring what's happening inside of you. You learn how to encourage others while feeling empty. You learn how to smile in public and struggle in private. And because you've been doing it for so long, it starts to feel normal.

You also start to believe that God expects this from you. You think faith means endurance. You think obedience means sacrifice without rest. I mean, if you are like me, you think being strong means never admitting when something hurts. So, when things get heavy, you pray, push through, and keep moving, even when you don't understand why you're so exhausted.

At some point, though, something shifts. It might be a moment, a conversation, a breakdown, or just quiet realization. You begin to understand that surviving is not the same as living. That being busy is not the same as being healthy. That being faithful does not mean being worn down.

You start to see that peace isn't something you've been avoiding. It's something you've been postponing. Because choosing peace means making changes. It means setting boundaries. It means disappointing people. It means letting go of situations you've grown used to, even when they're hurting you. It means trusting God in ways that feel unfamiliar.

And that, now, that's uncomfortable.

You've learned how to function in chaos. You know how to manage stress. You know how to carry responsibility. But you were never taught how to rest without feeling guilty. You were never taught how to say no without explaining yourself. You were never taught how to choose yourself without feeling selfish.

Peace feels strange at first. It feels risky. It feels undeserved. It feels like something meant for other people, not you.

But over time, you begin to understand that God never asked you to live overwhelmed. He never asked you to neglect your health, your joy, or your emotional well-being in order to prove your faith. He never asked you to carry things that were never yours to hold.

Peace had to come first because everything else was costing you too much. Your energy. Your clarity. Your confidence. Your connection to God. You were giving your best to everyone else and leaving yourself with nothing.

This book is not about pretending life is easy. It's not about having perfect faith or perfect answers. It's about learning how to live in a way that doesn't require you to break yourself in the process.

It's about understanding that rest is not weakness. Boundaries are not disobedience. Healing is not selfish. Taking care of your spirit is part of honoring God.

Peace had to come first because without it, nothing else could truly grow.

This is where the journey begins. Not with perfection, but with honesty. Not with pressure, but with permission. Not with fear, but with faith.

If you opened this book, that speaks volumes louder that you could imagine, and it says you are ready to start the journey of your Peace over Burdens.

PART 1: The Weight

1.

When Carrying Became Normal

You don't really notice when it starts. Most of the time, it begins with you stepping in because something needs to be done and you know you can do it. Someone needs help. Something falls apart. A responsibility gets dropped in your lap. You pick it up without thinking too much about it.

At first, it feels manageable. You tell yourself it's only for now. Once things settle down, you'll get back to yourself. You'll rest. You'll breathe. You'll slow down, but, you keep moving and assume balance will come later.

People start depending on you. They see that you're consistent. That you show up. That you don't quit when things get uncomfortable. Over time, that becomes your reputation. You're the one who handles things. The one people call. The one they trust.

You don't always question it. Part of you likes being reliable. Part of you likes knowing you matter. Part of you doesn't want to disappoint anyone. So, when more gets placed on you, you take it.

You get good at adjusting. You shift your schedule. You rearrange your priorities. You push your own needs further down the list. You convince yourself you'll deal with them later.

When you feel overwhelmed, you pray and keep going. When you're tired, you tell yourself everyone gets tired. When you're frustrated, you remind yourself that things could be worse. You become skilled at talking yourself out of slowing down.

Without realizing it, you start carrying things that aren't yours. Other people's stress. Their expectations. Their disappointments. Their unfinished business. You hold space for everyone and leave very little for yourself.

Since you rarely say no, people assume you're okay. They assume you've got it. They assume you'll speak up if something is wrong. But you don't always. Sometimes you don't even realize how heavy things have become until you're already worn down.

You function. You show up. You handle what needs to be handled. You move from one responsibility to the next. You learn how to live on low energy and call it normal.

Being busy becomes familiar. Being tired becomes routine. Being overwhelmed becomes background noise.

And because you're still standing, you think you're fine.

But somewhere deep down, you know you're carrying more than you should. You feel it in your body. You feel it in your patience. You feel it in your prayers. You feel it in how little space you've left for rest, for joy, for yourself.

Still, you keep going.

That's what you've always done.

2.

Learning to Survive in Silence

At some point, you learn that not everything you're going through is safe to share. Some experiences are too complicated to explain. Some emotions feel too heavy to put into words. Some situations are easier to carry alone than to try to justify to other people.

So, you become quiet.

Not because you don't have anything to say, but because you've learned that not everyone knows how to listen. Some people minimize what you're feeling. Others rush to give advice before they understand the situation. Some turn your vulnerability into gossip. Others simply don't have the emotional capacity to hold space for you.

After a few disappointing experiences, you stop opening up the same way.

You start choosing carefully what parts of yourself you reveal. You learn how to answer, "How are you?" with something that sounds honest without being vulnerable. You learn how to smile through conversations while carrying things no one knows about.

Silence becomes protection.

It feels safer to process things privately than to risk being misunderstood. It feels easier to pray quietly than to explain your faith struggles to people who expect you to always be strong. It feels more manageable to journal, think, and cry alone than to invite someone into your pain and feel exposed.

Over time, this way of coping becomes automatic.

You stop reaching out when something hurts. You stop asking for help when you're overwhelmed. You convince yourself that you're fine handling things on your own. You tell yourself that everyone has problems and that yours aren't worth burdening others with.

On the surface, you appear composed. You handle your responsibilities. You show up where you're needed. You remain dependable. People admire your strength without realizing how much of it is built on unspoken struggles.

But surviving in silence comes with a cost.

When you don't express what you're feeling, it doesn't disappear. It settles inside you. It shows up in your body, your sleep, your patience, and your energy. It affects how you respond to stress. It shapes how you relate to people. It influences how close you allow others to get.

You may find yourself feeling emotionally distant at times, even with people you care about. Not because you don't love them, but because you've trained yourself to handle things internally. Letting someone see your weakness feels unfamiliar. Trusting someone with your pain feels risky.

So, you carry it quietly.

You pray. You reflect. You analyze. You try to make sense of things on your own. You search Scripture. You listen to sermons. You read encouraging words. You do everything you know how to do to stay grounded.

And many times, that inner work strengthens you.

It teaches you resilience. It deepens your faith. It helps you develop emotional awareness. It sharpens your discernment. You learn how to hear God's voice in quiet spaces. You learn how to sit with uncomfortable emotions instead of avoiding them.

But silence was never meant to be your permanent home.

God designed you for connection, not isolation. He created you to be supported, not just self-sufficient. He never intended for you to carry everything alone, even when you're capable.

There is a difference between privacy and isolation.

Privacy is choosing wisely who has access to your story.
Isolation is believing no one deserves access at all.

One protects you.
The other slowly drains you.

At some point, you must examine whether your silence is still serving you. Whether it is helping you heal or simply helping you hide. Whether it is preserving your peace or preventing deeper growth.

Learning to survive in silence may have gotten you through difficult seasons. It may have helped you stay functional when life felt overwhelming. It may have been the only option you had at certain times.

But survival is not the same as wholeness.

Strength does not mean never needing support.

Faith does not mean carrying everything alone.

Maturity is knowing when to be quiet and when to reach out.

There is wisdom in discernment. Not everyone deserves your vulnerability. Not everyone is safe. But God will always provide the right people when you are willing to receive them.

You do not have to perform strength to be respected. You do not have to hide pain to be valued, and You do not have to struggle alone to be faithful.

Learning when to speak is just as important as learning when to be silent.

And peace begins to grow when you allow yourself to be honest in the right spaces.

3.

The Strength No One Saw

Most people only see what you allow them to see.

They see you showing up. They see you handling responsibilities. They see you staying composed in difficult situations. They see you smiling, working, serving, and moving forward. From the outside, it looks like confidence. It looks like stability. It looks like strength.

What they don't see is everything it takes for you to keep doing that.

They don't see the mornings when you wake up already tired. The days when you have to talk yourself into getting out of bed. The moments when your mind feels heavy before anything has even gone wrong. The prayers you whisper quietly because you don't have the energy to explain what you're feeling.

They don't see how much emotional work you do just to stay grounded.

You regulate your reactions. You monitor your tone. You choose your words carefully. You hold back tears. You manage disappointment. You keep yourself together in spaces where falling apart would feel unsafe or inconvenient.

That takes strength.

You don't make a habit of telling people when things are hard. Not because you're dishonest, but because you've learned that everyone is carrying something. You don't want to add to anyone else's load. You don't want to be seen as needy, dramatic, or unstable. So you process quietly.

You pray privately. You reflect internally. You sort through your thoughts on your own. You work through confusion without an audience. You wrestle with questions about faith, purpose, and direction in silence.

That takes strength.

You keep loving even when you've been disappointed. You keep trusting even after being let down. You keep believing in people even when they haven't always shown up for you. You choose not to become bitter. You choose not to harden your heart.

That takes strength.

There have been seasons when you were holding things together with faith and determination alone. Seasons when you felt unsure, unappreciated, or emotionally drained, but still showed up anyway. Seasons when quitting would have been easier than continuing, but you kept going.

Not because you were fearless.
Because you were committed.

Committed to your calling, to your values, or to your healing. Committed to honoring God with your life.

And that commitment carried you through moments no one knows about.

You learned how to be strong without becoming cold. How to be resilient without becoming detached. How to protect your heart without closing it completely. How to survive without losing your softness.

That balance is not accidental. It is developed through prayer, reflection, and intentional growth.

Still, there are times when you wonder if anyone truly sees the work you do behind the scenes. The emotional labor. The spiritual discipline. The personal sacrifices. The inner battles. The quiet victories.

Sometimes it feels like your strength is taken for granted.

But God sees it.

He sees every time you chose patience instead of reacting. Every time you chose forgiveness instead of resentment. Every time you chose faith instead of fear. Every time you chose peace instead of chaos.

Nothing you've done to stay whole has been wasted.

Listen, Strength is not only found in loud moments. It is found in consistency. In character. In the daily decision to keep growing, even when no one is applauding.

You don't have to perform your strength for it to be real.

You don't have to explain your journey for it to matter.

You don't have to prove how far you've come.

The fact that you are still standing, still believing, still healing, and still becoming is evidence enough.

And that strength deserves to be honored, especially by you.

4.

Smiling Through the Storm

There comes a point in life when you realize that how you carry yourself matters.

Not in a superficial way. In a practical one.

Your reputation affects your opportunities. Your consistency affects your credibility. Your attitude affects how people receive you. Whether you like it or not, people form opinions based on what they see.

So, you learn early how to manage your presentation.

You learn how to walk into professional spaces prepared, even when your personal life is unsettled. You learn how to speak clearly when you're processing things privately. You learn how to stay focused on your goals when distractions are pulling at you from every direction.

This isn't about pretending.

It's about stewardship. Stewardship of your calling. Stewardship of your gifts, and stewardship of your future.

There were seasons when things behind the scenes were uncertain. Decisions were heavy. Direction wasn't always clear. Yet you still showed up prepared. You still did your work with excellence. You still treated people with respect, and still honored your commitments.

That takes discipline.

Many people allow personal storms to disrupt their purpose. They abandon goals. They damage relationships. They burn bridges. They lose momentum.

You didn't.

You learned how to separate temporary emotions from long-term vision. You learned how to protect what you were building.

You understood that every setback didn't need an audience. Every frustration didn't need commentary. Every struggle didn't need to be explained.

Some things were handled privately, with God.

That wasn't avoidance, that was wisdom.

You learned how to pray in private and perform with excellence in public. You learned how to cry in prayer and walk into meetings with clarity. You learned how to process disappointment and still deliver quality. That balance is rare.

It's easy to fall apart publicly, but it's harder to stay grounded quietly.

But here's the tension.

When you live in "performance mode" too long, you can forget to rest.

When you're always focused on maintaining stability, you can neglect your emotional needs.

When you're committed to excellence, you can ignore exhaustion.

Maturity requires reflection. It requires asking yourself whether you're still managing well or just managing, whether you're still healthy or just functional, and whether you're still aligned, or just surviving.

God honors excellence, discipline, and integrity. But He also honors rest, honesty, and restoration.

Smiling through storms is not about denying reality, it's about refusing to let chaos define your character, and learning when to release the storm in God's presence, so that you can keep building with peace.

5.

When Faith Felt Fragile

There comes a point in life when faith begins to feel different. Not because belief has disappeared, and not because God has failed, but because experience has changed the way trust works. When you are younger in faith, prayer feels simple. You ask, you believe, and you move forward. There is confidence in not knowing too much. There is comfort in assuming things will work out the way you hope.

As life becomes more complex, faith becomes more complex too. Responsibilities increase. Disappointments happen. Prayers are not always answered quickly, and sometimes they are not answered in the way you expected. You begin to notice that trusting God requires more than repeating familiar words. It requires patience, emotional endurance, and a willingness to sit with uncertainty.

I know what that season feels like. It is the season where you are still praying and still believing, but you are also tired of carrying unanswered questions. You are still encouraging others, but quietly wishing someone would encourage you. You are still showing up in faith spaces, but feeling less confident than you once did. Nothing is broken, but nothing feels effortless anymore either.

During that time, prayer changes. It becomes less formal and more honest. You stop trying to sound strong and start telling God exactly how you feel. Instead of hiding disappointment, you bring it to Him. Instead of pretending you understand everything, you admit when you do not. You begin to realize that real faith is not about pretending to be unshaken. It is about staying connected even when you are unsure.

This is also when many people struggle privately. They worry that having questions means they are failing spiritually. They think feeling discouraged means their faith is weak. They assume that strong believers are never confused. But that is not true. Mature faith includes reflection. It includes moments of doubt, wrestling, and reevaluation. It includes learning how to trust God without needing constant reassurance.

What often goes unnoticed is how much strength it takes to remain faithful in those seasons. It takes strength to keep praying when you feel unheard. It takes strength to keep serving when you feel depleted. It takes strength to keep believing when circumstances suggest otherwise. That strength does not come from perfection. It comes from relationship.

Over time, you begin to understand that fragile faith is not broken faith. It is stretched faith. It is faith that has been tested by real life and still chooses to remain connected to God. It is faith that has moved beyond habit into intentional trust. It is faith that knows how to wait, how to listen, and how to surrender control.

Looking back, those seasons often become turning points. They deepen your prayer life. They sharpen your discernment. They teach you how to lean on God without depending on emotional highs. They help you develop a faith that is steady rather than dramatic, consistent rather than conditional.

You come out of that season with a quieter confidence. You may not have all the answers, but you have clarity. You may not feel invincible, but you feel anchored. You learn that faith does not have to feel strong every day to be real. It simply has to remain rooted.

And that kind of faith lasts.

6.

Praying While Breaking

There are seasons when prayer feels strong and confident. You know what you believe. You know what you are asking for. You feel steady in your faith. Even when things are difficult, you trust that God is working.

And then there are seasons when you are praying while quietly falling apart.

You are still talking to God. You are still reading Scripture. You are still saying "amen" and "thank You" and "I trust You." But underneath all of that, you are tired. You are discouraged. You are uncertain. You are trying to hold yourself together while asking God to hold everything else.

I know that season well.

It is the season where you pray out of discipline more than emotion. You show up in prayer because you know you need to, not because you feel strong. Sometimes your prayers are short. Sometimes they are repetitive. Sometimes they are just honest conversations with God where you admit that you do not know what else to say.

During that time, prayer becomes less about sounding spiritual and more about survival.

You stop trying to impress God with perfect words. You stop pretending that everything is fine. You bring Him your confusion, your frustration, your disappointment, and your exhaustion. You tell Him when you are scared. You tell Him when you are angry. You tell Him when you feel weak.

And slowly, you learn that God is not offended by any of it.

We are often taught, directly or indirectly, that strong faith means confident prayer. Those mature believers always sound hopeful. That spiritual people never feel overwhelmed. But real faith does not work that way. Real faith shows up even when it feels messy.

There were times when I prayed and still cried afterward. Times when I asked God for clarity and still felt unsure. Times when I asked for peace and still felt restless. At first, I wondered if something was wrong with me. I questioned whether I was praying correctly. I worried that my emotions meant I was failing spiritually.

They did not.

They meant I was human.

Praying while breaking teaches you how to be honest with God in a deeper way. It strips away performance. It removes religious language that no longer fits your reality. It forces you to rely on relationship instead of routine.

You begin to understand that God does not need you to be strong for Him to hear you. He does not need you to have everything figured out before you come to Him. He does not require polished prayers. He desires real ones.

In those seasons, prayer becomes your anchor. Not because it fixes everything immediately, but because it keeps you connected. It reminds you that you are not walking through difficulty alone. It gives you somewhere safe to release what you cannot carry by yourself.

Over time, you also learn patience.

You learn that some answers come slowly.
Some healing takes time.
Some breakthroughs happen quietly.

You learn how to trust God in the waiting. You learn how to keep praying even when progress feels invisible. You learn how to rest in His presence instead of constantly searching for signs.

Looking back, those seasons often become sacred. They reshape your relationship with God. They deepen your understanding of grace. They teach you that faith is not about always being okay. It is about always staying connected.

You come out of those seasons stronger, not because you avoided pain, but because you met God inside of it.

7.

The Cost of Always Being Strong

For a long time, I believed being strong meant being reliable. It meant not letting personal struggles interfere with responsibilities. It meant keeping commitments, meeting expectations, and handling situations without drawing unnecessary attention to myself. That mindset helped me build a life that looked stable from the outside, and in many ways, it served me well.

But over time, I started noticing patterns that I had ignored.

I noticed that I rarely asked for help, even when it was available. I noticed that I had a habit of saying yes automatically, before considering whether I actually had the capacity. I noticed that I felt uncomfortable depending on other people, even in healthy relationships. Somewhere along the way, independence had turned into isolation.

Let me be honest. I did not realize how much that was shaping my life.

Because I was used to handling things on my own, I often assumed others would do the same. I expected people to manage their emotions, responsibilities, and problems without much support. When they didn't, I sometimes felt frustrated without fully understanding why. Looking back now, I can see that my expectations were shaped by my own coping habits.

Being strong also affected how I made decisions. I learned to prioritize what needed to be done over what I needed emotionally. I chose practicality over rest. I chose stability over vulnerability. I chose consistency over honesty. Most of the time, those choices felt responsible. In reality, they were often rooted in fear — fear of disappointing others, fear of losing momentum, fear of appearing weak.

We do that sometimes, don't we?

We call it discipline.
We call it maturity.
We call it wisdom.

But sometimes it's just survival dressed up nicely.

Over time, that way of living begins to affect your relationships. People may see you as dependable, but they may not always feel close to you. You become someone others respect, but not always someone they truly know. You share selectively. You reveal carefully. You keep parts of yourself protected.

Not because you're hiding.

Because you've learned that being "together" keeps life manageable.

The cost also shows up in your body and mind. You begin to live in a constant state of alertness. You're always thinking ahead, preparing for what could go wrong, managing potential problems before they happen. Rest becomes something you schedule instead of something you experience. Peace becomes something you work for instead of something you receive.

I had to confront that in myself.

I had to admit that I didn't always know how to slow down without feeling irresponsible. I had to recognize that I equated rest with laziness and vulnerability with risk. I had to unlearn the belief that my value came from how much I could handle.

That process wasn't comfortable.

It required me to rethink what strength actually meant.

Strength is not avoiding dependence.
Strength is choosing healthy interdependence.

Strength is not carrying everything alone.
Strength is knowing when to invite support.

Strength is not being emotionally unavailable.
Strength is learning how to be present.

God never intended for strength to cost you connection, clarity, or peace. He never designed you to live in constant self-protection mode. He created you for community, balance, and rest as much as for purpose and responsibility.

Learning that changed how I live.

It changed how I relate to people.
It changed how I manage my energy.
It changed how I make decisions.
It changed how I pray.

I no longer measure success by how much I can carry. I measure it by how well I can live, love, and remain grounded in God's presence.

And that shift made all the difference.

PART 2: THE STRUGGLE WITHIN

8.

Quiet Battles No One Knew

Some of the hardest seasons in life are the ones no one ever sees. There is no public crisis, no dramatic announcement, and no obvious sign that anything is wrong. From the outside, everything looks normal. You are working, showing up, meeting responsibilities, and staying connected. But internally, you are navigating questions, emotional shifts, and personal adjustments that very few people know about.

Looking back now, I realize how many of my most important battles happened quietly. There were moments when I questioned decisions I had already made and wondered whether I was moving in the right direction or simply moving out of habit. There were times when I felt uncertain about paths I had chosen and unsure about what was coming next. Those thoughts were not rooted in insecurity as much as they were rooted in growth. Growth often begins with discomfort, and that discomfort usually happens in private.

We do not always talk about that part of the journey. We talk about breakthroughs, victories, and blessings, but we rarely talk about the silent seasons when you are trying to realign your life without making everything public. During those times, much of the work happens internally. It happens in prayer, in reflection, and in honest conversations with yourself about what needs to change and what needs to stay.

Well, you know how that goes. Those late-night thoughts, those quiet moments in the car, and those prayers whispered when no one is around are often where the real transformation begins. Many people assume strength is loud and visible, connected to leadership, confidence, and success. In reality, some of the strongest moments in your life happen when no one is watching. They happen when you choose restraint instead of reacting, wisdom instead of revenge, and healing instead of denial.

I had to learn how to do that without applause. I had to confront emotional patterns that were familiar but unhealthy and admit when I was holding on to things out of comfort rather than conviction. That level of honesty was uncomfortable, but it was necessary. It forced me to take responsibility for my own growth instead of blaming circumstances or waiting for things to change on their own.

Quiet struggles also teach you discernment. Over time, you learn who you can talk to and who you cannot. You learn when to share and when to stay silent. You learn how to protect your healing process from unnecessary opinions and distractions. You learn how to be private without becoming closed off. That balance takes time, and it is usually developed through trial and error.

There were moments when I wanted to explain myself and justify my choices. I wanted people to understand why I was changing and why certain decisions mattered to me. Eventually, I learned that not every transition needs an explanation. Some seasons are meant to be between you and God. Some growth is personal before it is public, and that is not something to apologize for.

In those quiet spaces, God often does His deepest work. He reshapes your perspective, challenges assumptions, clarifies priorities, and strengthens your identity. None of that happens loudly. It happens through consistency, reflection, and obedience. It happens when you choose to keep growing even when no one is cheering you on.

Over time, you begin to trust yourself more, not in a prideful way, but in a grounded way. You learn how to listen to your spirit, recognize when something is off, honor your boundaries, and move with intention instead of impulse. Those skills are developed in silence, through experience and self-awareness.

When people later notice your growth, they may assume it happened suddenly. They may think you simply changed overnight. They may not realize how many internal battles were fought before anything shifted outward. But you know. You know how much prayer it took, how much restraint it required, how much courage it demanded, and how much humility it involved.

Those quiet struggles did not weaken you. They strengthened you. They taught you how to stand from the inside out, and that inner strength is what carries you forward.

9.

Unanswered Prayers

There are moments in life when you pray with full expectation. You believe in what you are asking for. You have faith that God hears you. You trust that He is able. You speak His promises. You stand on His Word. You do everything you know how to do spiritually, emotionally, and practically.

And still, nothing happens.

At least, nothing happens the way you hoped it would.

Those seasons can be confusing, especially when you are sincere in your faith. You are not being careless. You are not being inconsistent. You are not treating God casually. You are doing your part. You are praying. You are waiting. You are trying to remain obedient. Yet the door stays closed. The situation remains unresolved. The answer does not come.

Let me be honest. That is one of the hardest places to sit.

It is difficult to reconcile strong faith with delayed outcomes. It is challenging to trust God fully while quietly wondering why something has not changed. You start asking yourself questions you never thought you would ask. Am I missing something? Am I doing something wrong? Am I being overlooked? Is God hearing me?

We have all been there.

Unanswered prayers have a way of testing not just what you believe, but how you believe. They force you to examine whether your faith is rooted in relationship or in results. They reveal whether you trust God only when things are going well, or even when they are unclear.

During those seasons, prayer often becomes more personal. You stop repeating general phrases and start speaking honestly. You tell God when you are disappointed. You admit when you are tired of waiting. You confess when you feel discouraged. You ask for strength instead of shortcuts. You ask for peace instead of control.

I had to learn how to do that.

For a long time, I believed that strong faith meant never questioning anything. I thought trusting God meant always being confident and calm. But over time, I learned that real faith includes honesty. It includes moments of frustration, confusion, and even silence. It includes staying connected even when you do not understand what God is doing.

Unanswered prayers also teach patience in a way nothing else can.

Waiting stretches you. It exposes impatience. It reveals attachment. It forces you to confront areas where you want control more than clarity. Sometimes you realize that what you were asking for was not wrong, but the timing was not right. Other times, you learn that what you wanted was good, but not what God had planned.

That is not easy to accept.

Especially when you have invested emotionally, spiritually, and practically into something. Especially when you have done everything "right." Especially when the outcome matters deeply to you.

Still, God's silence is not absence. Sometimes it is protection. Sometimes it is preparation. Sometimes it is redirection. Sometimes it is refinement.

We do not always know which one it is in the moment. We often only understand later, when we can see the full picture.

Looking back now, I can identify prayers that were not answered the way I wanted but were answered in ways that ultimately protected me. Situations I thought I needed that would have limited me.

Opportunities I wanted that would have distracted me. Relationships I prayed for that would have cost me my peace.

At the time, it felt like loss.

Later, it felt like grace.

Unanswered prayers also teach you how to trust God's character, not just His power. They remind you that He is not only capable, but wise. Not only strong, but intentional. Not only loving, but strategic. They invite you to believe that God sees what you cannot see and knows what you do not know.

That kind of trust is developed, not inherited. It grows through disappointment. It deepens through waiting. It matures through surrender.

Eventually, you reach a place where your prayers change again. You still ask. You still hope. You still believe. But you also surrender more easily. You learn how to say, "God, I want this, but I trust You more." You learn how to release outcomes without releasing faith.

And that is freedom.

Unanswered prayers do not mean you are forgotten. They do not mean you are unworthy. They do not mean God is distant. Often, they mean

He is doing something deeper than you can see in the moment.

Something in you. Something around you. Something ahead of you.

And when you finally understand that, waiting becomes less painful, trust becomes more natural, and peace becomes more consistent.

10.

When Trust was Unshaken

Trust in God does not always look the way people expect it to. Many assume that trusting God means feeling calm all the time, being confident in every situation, and never questioning outcomes. In reality, trust is often practiced in moments of uncertainty, disappointment, and waiting. It is built quietly through consistent decisions to believe God's character even when circumstances are unclear.

There are seasons when life does not offer easy reassurance. Plans change. Doors close. Relationships shift. Opportunities fall through. Prayers remain unanswered. During those times, trust is not something you feel naturally. It is something you choose intentionally. You decide to continue believing in God's wisdom even when you do not understand His timing. You choose to remain obedient even when the outcome is uncertain. You commit to faithfulness even when emotions fluctuate.

I have learned that unshaken trust is not rooted in perfection. It is rooted in experience. It grows through seeing God provide in unexpected ways, protect you from things you did not recognize as harmful, and redirect you toward paths you never would have chosen on your own. Over time, those experiences create a quiet confidence that does not depend on constant confirmation.

Many people struggle with trust because they confuse faith with comfort. They believe that if God is truly working, everything should feel peaceful and predictable. But spiritual maturity teaches you that growth often happens in uncomfortable spaces. Trust develops when you continue to walk forward without knowing every detail. It deepens when you learn how to release control and accept that God's perspective is greater than your own.

One of the most important lessons in developing unshaken trust is learning how to separate outcomes from identity. When things do not work out, it is easy to internalize disappointment and begin questioning your worth, your purpose, or your spiritual standing. Mature faith reminds you that unanswered prayers and delayed breakthroughs do not diminish your value or negate God's favor. They are often part of a larger process that is still unfolding.

Trust also requires consistency. It is reinforced through daily practices such as prayer, reflection, Scripture, and intentional obedience. These habits create spiritual stability that carries you through uncertain seasons. When challenges arise, you are not starting from nothing. You are standing on a foundation that has already been built.

Over time, you begin to notice a shift in how you respond to difficulties. You no longer panic as easily. You no longer rush to control outcomes. You become more patient in waiting and more discerning in decision-making. You learn how to listen before reacting and how to seek God's direction before taking action. That shift is evidence of spiritual growth.

Unshaken trust does not mean that you never feel disappointed or discouraged. It means that those emotions no longer control your decisions. It means that even when you feel uncertain, you remain grounded. Even when answers are delayed, you remain faithful. Even when situations are challenging, you remain committed to walking in integrity.

Looking back now, I can see that the seasons that strengthened my trust were not the easiest ones. They were the ones that required surrender, patience, and humility. They were the ones that taught me how to depend on God without demanding explanations. They were the ones that shaped my character and clarified my priorities.

Trust that is unshaken is not loud. It does not need constant validation. It does not rely on public affirmation. It is quiet, steady, and rooted in relationship. It is built over time through obedience, reflection, and lived experience.

And that kind of trust becomes one of your greatest sources of strength.

11.

Carrying Other People's Pain

One of the quiet responsibilities that comes with being dependable, compassionate, and spiritually grounded is that people tend to bring their struggles to you. Sometimes they do it intentionally, and sometimes it happens naturally. They trust your judgment. They feel safe with you. They believe you can handle what they are going through. Over time, you become someone others lean on during difficult moments.

At first, that feels meaningful. It feels like purpose. It feels like confirmation that your life, your experiences, and your growth are useful to someone else. You listen. You advise. You encourage. You pray. You support. You make yourself available. You do it because you care and because you understand what it means to need someone.

But eventually, if you are not careful, that role can become heavy.

Carrying other people's pain is not the same as supporting them. Supporting someone means walking with them while maintaining your own emotional stability. Carrying their pain means absorbing their stress, their anxiety, their disappointment, and their unresolved trauma as if it were your own. It happens slowly, often without you realizing it. You think about their problems when you are alone. You feel responsible for their outcomes. You worry about situations you cannot control. You replay conversations in your mind, wondering if you said enough or did enough.

Well, you know how that goes.

When you care deeply, it is easy to cross that line.

Many people who struggle with this are natural helpers. They are empathetic. They are perceptive. They notice emotional shifts. They pick up on unspoken tension. They sense when something is wrong. Those qualities are gifts, but without boundaries, they can become burdens.

Over time, constantly carrying other people's emotional weight affects your clarity. You become mentally distracted. You feel emotionally drained. You find it harder to separate your own needs from everyone else's. You may even begin to neglect your own healing because you are focused on helping others manage theirs.

I had to learn that compassion without boundaries leads to burnout.

There is a difference between being available and being responsible. You can care deeply without trying to fix everything. You can listen without taking ownership of someone else's choices. You can pray without feeling personally accountable for the outcome. That balance takes wisdom, maturity, and self-awareness.

Sometimes, people do not want solutions. They want validation. Sometimes they do not want direction. They want comfort. Sometimes they do not want accountability. They want reassurance. If you are not careful, you can find yourself giving more than is healthy simply to keep people emotionally stable.

That is not sustainable.

Carrying other people's pain also affects how you show up in your own life. You may become emotionally unavailable because your capacity is already full. You may feel guilty resting because others are struggling. You may minimize your own challenges because someone else "has it worse." Over time, that mindset trains you to dismiss your own emotional needs.

That is not wisdom. That is self-neglect.

Learning to release emotional responsibility is not selfish. It is necessary. It allows you to serve from a place of strength instead of exhaustion. It allows you to remain present without becoming overwhelmed. It allows you to help without losing yourself.

God never called you to replace Him in people's lives. He did not assign you the role of savior, rescuer, or emotional anchor. He called you to love, encourage, and support, while trusting Him to do the deeper work.

That understanding brings freedom.

You learn how to care without carrying.
You learn how to listen without absorbing.
You learn how to love without losing balance.

As you grow in that area, your relationships become healthier. Your energy becomes more stable. Your mind becomes clearer. Your faith becomes more grounded. You stop operating from obligation and start operating from wisdom.

Carrying other people's pain is something many strong, compassionate people struggle with. But learning how to release it is part of emotional and spiritual maturity.

12.

The Weight of Expectations

Expectations shape more of our lives than we often realize. Some are spoken clearly. Others are implied. Some come from family, friends, and communities. Others come from professional environments, faith spaces, and social circles. And some of the heaviest expectations are the ones we place on ourselves.

Over time, those expectations begin to influence how you make decisions, how you measure success, and how you evaluate your worth. You start considering not only what you want or need, but how your choices will be perceived. You become mindful of who might be disappointed, who might question you, and who might feel affected. Without realizing it, you begin carrying multiple narratives about who you are supposed to be.

Many people learn early how to meet expectations. They learn how to perform well, behave responsibly, and adapt quickly. They become reliable. They become consistent. They become dependable. Those traits are often praised and rewarded, so they continue strengthening them. Over time, meeting expectations becomes part of their identity.

The challenge is that expectations rarely stay reasonable.

What begins as appreciation turns into assumption. What begins as support turns into pressure. What begins as trust turns into dependency. People grow accustomed to your reliability and begin expecting it without considering your capacity. They assume you will always show up, always understand, always accommodate, and always adjust.

Well, you know how that goes.

You become "the one" people count on, and slowly, the margin in your life begins to disappear.

At the same time, internal expectations intensify. You expect yourself to stay composed. You expect yourself to be productive. You expect yourself to remain spiritually grounded, emotionally stable, financially responsible, and relationally available. You expect yourself to grow without stumbling and lead without resting. When you fall short, you become self-critical rather than compassionate.

That mindset is exhausting.

Living under constant expectation creates quiet anxiety. You may not feel overwhelmed in dramatic ways, but you feel pressure to maintain consistency. You feel responsible for outcomes. You feel uneasy when you consider slowing down or changing direction. You begin measuring your value by performance rather than presence.

Over time, this affects how you experience life. Joy becomes conditional. Rest feels undeserved. Celebration feels postponed. You tell yourself you will relax later, enjoy later, breathe later, after everything is handled. Later becomes a moving target that never quite arrives.

I had to confront that pattern in myself.

I had to recognize how much of my motivation was driven by approval, responsibility, and fear of disappointing others. I had to admit that I sometimes made choices based on expectation rather than alignment. That realization was uncomfortable, but necessary.

Healthy expectations encourage growth. Unhealthy expectations restrict it.

There is nothing wrong with being dependable. There is nothing wrong with being committed. There is nothing wrong with being responsible. The problem arises when those qualities become obligations rather than choices. When you feel trapped by the image others have of you. When you feel pressured to maintain a version of yourself that no longer reflects where you are.

Learning to manage expectations requires discernment and courage. You have to decide which expectations are reasonable and which are unrealistic. You have to learn how to communicate boundaries clearly. You have to accept that some people will be disappointed when you change, grow, or prioritize your well-being.

That discomfort is part of maturity.

Releasing excessive expectations does not mean lowering standards. It means realigning them. It means allowing yourself to evolve without guilt. It means choosing sustainability over constant performance. It means trusting that your worth is not dependent on constant output.

Over time, you learn how to operate from clarity rather than pressure. You learn how to say yes with intention and no without apology. You learn how to pursue excellence without sacrificing peace. You learn how to honor commitments while honoring yourself.

That balance is not automatic. It is developed through experience, reflection, and self-awareness.

And once you learn it, life becomes lighter.

Not because responsibility disappears, but because it is no longer carried alone.

13.

Learning to Say NO

For many people, learning to say no is far more difficult than learning to say yes. Saying yes often feels polite, responsible, and cooperative. It feels like the right thing to do. It maintains peace. It avoids conflict. It keeps relationships smooth. Over time, saying yes becomes a habit, especially for people who are dependable, empathetic, and spiritually grounded.

Most of us were not taught how to decline gracefully. We were taught how to accommodate, adjust, and sacrifice. We learned early that being agreeable earned approval and that being available built trust. Those lessons are not wrong, but when they are not balanced, they create patterns that are hard to break.

Eventually, constant agreement begins to take a toll.

You start committing to things you do not have the energy for. You agree to responsibilities that stretch you thin. You rearrange your schedule to accommodate others while neglecting your own needs. You convince yourself that you will rest later, after this one more obligation is handled.

That pattern repeats itself until exhaustion feels normal.

Well, you know how that goes.

You tell yourself it is temporary. You tell yourself you are just helping out. You tell yourself it will balance out eventually. Meanwhile, your capacity keeps shrinking.

One of the reasons saying no feels uncomfortable is because it challenges expectations. When people are used to you being available, your absence feels personal to them. When people are used to you accommodating, your boundaries feel unfamiliar. Sometimes they interpret your no as rejection, disinterest, or selfishness, even when it is simply honesty.

That fear keeps many people silent.

They would rather overextend than disappoint. They would rather be tired than misunderstood. They would rather sacrifice peace than have difficult conversations.

Learning to say no requires emotional maturity. It means understanding that discomfort is sometimes necessary for healthy relationships. It means recognizing that every yes is also a no to something else, whether that is rest, family time, personal growth, or spiritual renewal. It means accepting that you cannot meet every need without neglecting your own.

I had to learn that boundaries are not barriers. They are structures that protect what matters.

When you begin practicing intentional refusal, you become more aware of your priorities. You start evaluating requests based on alignment rather than obligation. You ask yourself whether something fits your values, your season, and your capacity. You stop responding automatically and start responding thoughtfully.

At first, that feels awkward.

You may overexplain. You may feel guilty. You may rehearse conversations in your head before speaking. You may worry about how others will respond. That is normal. Boundary-setting is a skill, and like any skill, it improves with practice.

Over time, something shifts.

You realize that the people who truly respect you will adjust. They may be surprised at first, but they will learn to honor your limits. You also learn that some relationships were built more on convenience than connection. Those relationships often change when boundaries are introduced.

That is part of growth.

Saying no also strengthens your sense of self. It reinforces that your time, energy, and presence are valuable. It reminds you that you are allowed to choose where you invest yourself. It teaches you how to lead your life intentionally rather than reactively.

From a faith perspective, learning to say no is also an act of stewardship. It reflects an understanding that your resources are entrusted to you and must be managed wisely. You cannot pour endlessly without being refilled. You cannot serve effectively while depleted. You cannot lead well while overwhelmed.

Healthy no's create space for better yeses.

They make room for rest, reflection, family, purpose, and spiritual growth. They allow you to show up fully where you are truly called, rather than partially everywhere.

Learning to say no is not about becoming distant or rigid. It is about becoming discerning. It is about honoring your limits while remaining compassionate. It is about choosing sustainability over burnout.

14.

When Rest Felt like Failure

For a long time, rest felt uncomfortable to me. It did not feel refreshing or restorative. It felt irresponsible. It felt unnecessary. It felt like something I had not earned yet. I associated rest with unfinished work and unfulfilled obligations. If there was still something to do, someone to help, or a goal to pursue, slowing down felt like falling behind.

That mindset develops quietly. It is shaped by environments that reward productivity and praise endurance. It is reinforced by expectations that value output more than balance. Over time, you begin to believe that being busy is a sign of commitment and that slowing down is a sign of weakness. Without realizing it, you start measuring your worth by how much you accomplish.

Many people live this way for years.

They move from one responsibility to the next without pause. They schedule every available hour. They multitask constantly. They push through exhaustion because stopping feels uncomfortable. Even when they have free time, they struggle to enjoy it because their minds remain occupied with unfinished tasks.

Well, you know how that goes.

You sit down to rest, but you cannot relax. You think about what still needs to be done. You mentally replay conversations. You plan tomorrow's schedule. You scroll through messages. You check emails. Your body is still, but your mind is working overtime.

Over time, this creates a distorted relationship with rest. Instead of seeing it as necessary, you view it as optional. Instead of seeing it as healthy, you view it as indulgent. Instead of seeing it as obedience, you view it as avoidance. You begin believing that only exhaustion proves dedication.

I had to confront that belief.

I had to recognize how much of my drive was rooted in fear rather than purpose. Fear of falling behind. Fear of losing momentum. Fear of disappointing others. Fear of being seen as less committed. That fear kept me in constant motion, even when my body and spirit were asking for pause.

Rest, however, is not a reward for finishing everything. It is a requirement for sustaining anything.

From a faith perspective, rest is not laziness. It is trust. It reflects confidence that God can work even when you are not actively striving. It acknowledges that your strength has limits and that His does not. Choosing rest is an act of humility. It is a decision to honor your humanity.

Learning that shifted my perspective.

I began to understand that rest protects clarity. It improves judgment. It strengthens emotional resilience. It deepens spiritual sensitivity. It preserves physical health. Without rest, even good work becomes distorted. Even meaningful service becomes burdensome. Even purpose becomes pressure.

There were moments when choosing rest felt like failure. It felt like I was letting something slip. It felt like I was being irresponsible. It felt like I was not doing enough. But over time, I learned that rest actually made me more effective, not less. It allowed me to return with focus instead of fatigue and with peace instead of pressure.

Rest also teaches boundaries.

It forces you to acknowledge that you cannot be everywhere, do everything, or carry everything. It reminds you that limits are not flaws. They are part of design. When you honor them, you operate with wisdom rather than pride.

As I grew in this area, I noticed changes in how I lived. I became more intentional with my energy. I became more selective with my commitments. I became more attentive in my relationships. I became more grounded in my faith. Rest created space for reflection, gratitude, and discernment.

Looking back now, I realize that learning to rest was part of learning to trust. It was part of learning to release control. It was part of learning to lead myself well.

Rest did not make me weaker.

It made me wiser. And that wisdom became one of the foundations of my peace.

PART 3: THE RELEASE

15.

Learning to Let Go

Letting go is one of the most misunderstood parts of personal and spiritual growth. Many people associate it with loss, weakness, or giving up. They assume that releasing something means it no longer mattered or that it was a mistake to care in the first place. Letting go is often a sign of maturity. It reflects an understanding that not everything is meant to stay in your life forever, even if it once served a meaningful purpose.

For a long time, I struggled with this concept. I believed that holding on was a form of loyalty. I thought endurance proved character. I assumed that walking away meant failure. As a result, I remained connected to situations, responsibilities, and expectations long after they had stopped being healthy. I convinced myself that patience would eventually turn discomfort into peace.

It rarely did.

Over time, I began noticing how much emotional energy was being consumed by things I could no longer change. Old disappointments. Unfulfilled expectations. Unresolved conversations. Relationships that had shifted. Opportunities that had passed. I carried them quietly, revisiting them in my thoughts and allowing them to influence my decisions long after their season had ended.

We all do this in different ways.

Some people hold on to regret.
Some hold on to resentment.
Some hold on to guilt.
Some hold on to old versions of themselves.

Holding on feels safer than releasing because it gives the illusion of control. It allows you to believe that if you keep thinking, analyzing, and revisiting something, you might eventually fix it. Letting go requires accepting that some things will never be fully resolved in the way you hoped.

That acceptance takes courage.

Learning to let go also means learning to grieve properly. Not every loss is dramatic. Some losses are subtle. They are the loss of expectations, routines, identities, and imagined futures. They still matter, even if no one else recognizes them. Pretending they do not hurt only delays healing.

I had to learn that acknowledging disappointment did not make me ungrateful. It made me honest. It allowed me to process emotions instead of suppressing them. It allowed me to move forward without carrying unnecessary weight.

Letting go also involves releasing unrealistic standards. Sometimes the hardest thing to release is the image of how you thought life would look. You must make peace with detours, delays, and changes in direction. You must accept that growth often requires adaptation rather than perfection.

From a faith perspective, letting go is closely connected to trust. It is choosing to believe that God can do more with your future than you can with your past. It is releasing control over outcomes and surrendering the need to understand everything immediately. It is recognizing that holding on too tightly can block new opportunities.

As I practiced letting go, I noticed a shift in my thinking. I became less reactive. I stopped replaying old situations as often. I became more present in my relationships. I approached decisions with clarity instead of fear. Releasing what no longer served me created space for what aligned with my purpose.

Letting go did not mean becoming detached or indifferent. It meant becoming intentional. It meant choosing peace over persistence in unhealthy patterns. It meant valuing emotional health over familiarity. It meant trusting myself enough to move forward.

Looking back now, I see that every major season of growth in my life required some form of release. Something had to be surrendered before something new could begin. That process was rarely easy, but it was always necessary.

Letting go is not about erasing the past. It is about learning from it without living in it. It is about honoring what was while making room for what is becoming.

And that is where true freedom begins.

16.

Laying it Down

There is a difference between knowing you need to release something and being willing to put it down. Most people understand the idea of letting go. They talk about moving on, healing, and starting fresh. But laying something down is more intentional than that. It means recognizing that you have been carrying something longer than you were meant to and choosing, consciously, to stop.

For a long time, I did not realize how much emotional weight I was managing every day. I was functioning. I was productive. I was showing up. On the surface, everything looked stable. But internally, I was holding on to old disappointments, unfinished conversations, unmet expectations, and responsibilities that no longer belonged to me. I had learned how to carry things quietly, so I assumed that meant I was handling them well.

I wasn't.

I was surviving them.

Some burdens are obvious. Financial pressure. Family responsibilities. Work demands. Health concerns. But others are more subtle. Emotional loyalty to people who no longer show up for you. Guilt over choices you made in past seasons. Pressure to maintain versions of yourself that no longer fit. Silent resentment that never found healthy expression. Those are the things that accumulate over time and begin to shape how you think, respond, and relate.

Well, you know how that happens.

You adjust.
You adapt.
You normalize it.

Until carrying becomes your default.

Laying things down requires you to pause long enough to notice what you are actually holding. It requires honesty with yourself about what is draining you. It requires acknowledging when self-reliance has turned into emotional isolation. It means admitting that strength has limits and that constantly managing everything is not sustainable.

I had to confront that in myself.

I had to accept that I did not need to carry every responsibility alone. I did not need to manage every outcome. I did not need to keep revisiting situations that were already over. I did not need to protect everyone else's comfort at the expense of my own peace.

Letting go of that mindset was uncomfortable.

It challenged my identity. It forced me to rethink what maturity looked like. It required me to trust that releasing control would not lead to collapse. It taught me that boundaries were not abandonment. They were clarity.

As I learned how to lay things down, my life became lighter. Not because problems disappeared, but because I stopped carrying what was never mine to manage. I became more intentional with my energy. I became more selective with my commitments. I became more present in my relationships. I stopped operating from obligation and started operating from alignment.

Laying things down also involves forgiveness. Not only forgiving others, but forgiving yourself. Forgiving yourself for staying too long. For trying too hard. For believing things would change when they did not. For carrying guilt that no longer served any purpose. That kind of forgiveness frees you from repeating emotional cycles.

Over time, you begin to recognize when something no longer belongs in your life. You become more aware of emotional attachments that limit growth. You learn how to release expectations that are unrealistic. You become more comfortable choosing peace over persistence in unhealthy patterns.

Looking back now, I can see that many of my breakthroughs happened after I finally laid something down. Not when I pushed harder. Not when I endured longer. But when I admitted that something had reached its limit and chose to release it.

That decision changed how I lived.

Laying it down is not about giving up. It is about choosing sustainability over burnout. It is about trusting that you do not have to carry every burden to prove your worth. It is about understanding that your strength is not measured by how much you endure, but by how wisely you manage your life.

When you learn how to do that, freedom becomes practical, not theoretical. It becomes something you experience daily, not something you hope for someday.

And that is when real release begins.

17.

Forgiving Without Excuses

Forgiveness is often discussed as a spiritual obligation or a moral requirement, but it is rarely presented as the complex emotional process that it actually is. Many people are told they should forgive quickly, move on easily, and avoid revisiting past hurt. In reality, forgiveness is rarely immediate, simple, or neat. It involves confronting pain honestly and choosing to release resentment without minimizing what happened.

For a long time, I struggled with this. I believed that forgiving meant pretending something did not affect me. I thought it required silence, emotional distance, and avoidance. If I did not talk about it, think about it, or acknowledge it, then I could convince myself I had moved on. What I was really doing, though, was suppressing unresolved feelings.

That approach never brings peace.

Avoidance creates emotional residue. It lingers beneath the surface and influences how you respond to people, how you build trust, and how you protect yourself. Over time, unresolved hurt turns into guardedness. You become more cautious. You share less. You expect disappointment. You begin anticipating harm even in healthy situations.

Forgiving without excuses requires honesty. It means acknowledging that something hurt, that it mattered, and that it changed you. It means refusing to minimize your experience in order to appear mature or spiritual. It means allowing yourself to feel disappointment, anger, and grief without letting those emotions control your future.

Many people excuse harmful behavior in the name of peace. They say things like, "They didn't mean it," "That's just how they are," or "I should be over it by now." Those statements may sound reasonable, but they often prevent true healing. They prioritize comfort over clarity and silence over resolution.

I had to learn that forgiving someone does not require justifying their actions.

You can release resentment while still recognizing responsibility. You can move forward without rewriting history. You can choose peace without erasing truth. Forgiveness is not denial. It is discernment.

Forgiving without excuses also means setting appropriate boundaries. Releasing bitterness does not require re-entering unhealthy situations.

Extending grace does not require tolerating repeated harm. Maturity teaches you how to balance compassion with wisdom.

Over time, I realized that forgiveness was more about my freedom than anyone else's. Holding onto anger kept me emotionally tied to situations that had already ended. Replaying hurtful moments kept me mentally invested in past seasons. Letting go allowed me to reclaim my energy and attention.

That shift was liberating.

Forgiveness also requires patience with yourself. Healing does not follow a timeline. Some wounds take longer to process than others. Some memories resurface unexpectedly. Some emotions return in waves. That does not mean you failed. It means you are human.

Learning to forgive without excuses teaches you emotional accountability. It helps you recognize when bitterness is forming and address it early. It strengthens your ability to communicate honestly. It improves the quality of your relationships. It deepens your self-awareness.

As you grow in this area, forgiveness becomes less about obligation and more about alignment. You forgive because resentment no longer fits who you are becoming. You release anger because it no longer serves your purpose. You choose peace because it supports your growth.

Looking back now, I see that forgiving without excuses was one of the most important steps in my healing. It allowed me to move forward without carrying emotional debt. It helped me rebuild trust in myself. It strengthened my capacity for healthy relationships.

Forgiveness, practiced honestly and wisely, does not weaken you.

It frees you.

18.

Boundaries and Breakthroughs

For a long time, I believed that personal growth came primarily from endurance. I thought breakthroughs happened when you stayed long enough, tried hard enough, prayed long enough, and sacrificed enough. I assumed that if I remained patient and faithful, eventually situations would improve on their own. What I did not understand was that growth often requires action, not just persistence.

One of the most important lessons I learned was that boundaries are not obstacles to progress. They are often the pathway to it.

Without boundaries, you remain emotionally available to situations that drain you. You stay connected to environments that limit your peace. You tolerate patterns that undermine your growth. You continue adjusting to dysfunction instead of addressing it. Over time, that constant accommodation weakens your confidence and clouds your judgment.

Well, you know how that works.

You start telling yourself that it's temporary. You convince yourself that things will shift eventually.

You justify staying uncomfortable because leaving feels complicated. Meanwhile, your emotional and mental energy keeps being depleted.

I had to confront the truth that my lack of boundaries was delaying my breakthrough.

Every time I avoided difficult conversations, I postponed clarity. Every time I ignored my limits, I reinforced unhealthy expectations. Every time I chose comfort over honesty, I extended cycles that needed to end. None of that felt dramatic in the moment. It felt practical. It felt peaceful. It felt responsible.

In reality, it was avoidance.

Boundaries require courage. They require you to speak up when silence feels easier. They require you to change patterns that others have grown comfortable with. They require you to accept that some people will resist your growth because it disrupts their access to you.

That resistance can be uncomfortable.

Some will misunderstand you. Some will challenge you. Some will question your intentions. Some will accuse you of changing. And they may be right.

You are changing.

You are learning how to honor your time.
You are learning how to protect your energy.
You are learning how to choose peace intentionally.

That is growth.

As I began establishing boundaries, I noticed shifts in every area of my life. My relationships became more honest. My schedule became more manageable. My thinking became clearer. My stress became more controlled. I stopped feeling guilty for prioritizing my well-being.

Boundaries also strengthened my faith. They taught me how to trust God with outcomes instead of trying to manage everything myself. They reminded me that obedience sometimes looks like stepping back instead of pressing forward. They helped me understand that preserving peace is part of spiritual maturity.

Breakthroughs often come after boundaries are set.

Not before.

After.

After you stop tolerating what is unhealthy.
After you stop negotiating your values.
After you stop minimizing your needs.

When you choose clarity over comfort, momentum follows. When you choose honesty over avoidance, freedom follows. When you choose alignment over approval, peace follows.

Looking back now, I see that many of my biggest breakthroughs came after I finally said enough. Enough explaining. Enough overextending. Enough compromising. Enough waiting for others to change.

I chose to change.

That decision reshaped my life.

Boundaries are not about pushing people away. They are about creating space for healthier connection. They are about defining what is acceptable and what is not. They are about teaching others how to treat you by how you treat yourself.

And when you learn how to do that, breakthroughs stop being accidental.

They become intentional.

19.

Rebuilding from the Inside

Most people focus on building their lives from the outside first. They focus on appearance, achievement, stability, and structure. They work hard to establish careers, relationships, routines, and reputations. They invest energy into creating something that looks solid and successful. On the surface, it often works.

But external stability does not always reflect internal strength.

You can have everything in place and still feel unsettled. You can meet goals and still feel disconnected. You can appear confident and still struggle privately. That is because sustainable growth does not begin with circumstances. It begins with character, mindset, and emotional health.

I had to learn that the hard way.

For a long time, I focused on managing responsibilities and meeting expectations. I learned how to perform well under pressure. I learned how to stay composed. I learned how to adapt quickly. Those skills helped me function, but they did not always help me heal. I was building structure without strengthening the foundation.

Eventually, that imbalance shows up.

It appears in patterns of overworking. It appears in emotional exhaustion. It appears in strained relationships. It appears in difficulty resting or trusting. It appears in feeling successful but not fulfilled. Those are signs that something inside needs attention.

Building from the inside requires intentional self-examination. It means taking time to reflect on your beliefs, habits, reactions, and motivations. It means asking yourself why you respond the way you do. It means identifying what triggers stress, defensiveness, or withdrawal. It means recognizing emotional patterns that developed in earlier seasons and deciding whether they still serve you.

That work is uncomfortable.

It forces you to confront parts of yourself that are easier to ignore. It requires honesty without self-condemnation. It requires responsibility without shame. It invites growth without perfectionism.

One of the most important aspects of internal development is learning emotional regulation. This includes managing stress, communicating effectively, processing disappointment, and responding thoughtfully rather than impulsively. These skills influence every area of life, from relationships to leadership to spiritual growth.

Building from the inside also involves strengthening your sense of identity. You learn how to separate who you are from what you do. You stop measuring your worth by productivity, performance, or approval. You begin grounding your confidence in values, integrity, and purpose.

Over time, that internal stability creates external consistency.

You become less reactive and more reflective. You become less anxious and more intentional. You become more resilient and less easily discouraged. You learn how to navigate change without losing yourself.

From a faith perspective, this process is closely connected to spiritual maturity. It involves renewing your mind, deepening your relationship with God, and aligning your choices with His direction. It strengthens discernment and sharpens wisdom.

As I committed to internal growth, I noticed lasting changes. I became more selective with my energy. I became more honest in my relationships. I became more grounded in my decisions. I became more confident in my boundaries. I stopped building my life around survival and started building it around purpose.

Looking back now, I understand that everything I was trying to create externally required internal preparation first. Stability, peace, leadership, and influence all depend on foundation. Without internal alignment, success becomes fragile.

Building from the inside is not a one-time process. It is ongoing. It requires regular reflection, humility, and adjustment. But it is worth the effort.

Because when your foundation is strong, everything you build on top of it lasts.

20.

Trusting GOD Again

Trusting God is not something you learn once and carry effortlessly for the rest of your life. It is something that is tested, challenged, broken, rebuilt, and strengthened over time. It evolves through seasons of blessing, disappointment, loss, recovery, and growth. Most people do not talk about that part. They talk about faith as if it is always steady and consistent. In reality, faith is often shaped through struggle.

There were moments in my life when trusting God did not come easily.

One of the most defining seasons for me was in 2015, when I became pregnant after believing for a long time that I might not be able to conceive. At first, I was happy. I was hopeful. I saw it as a miracle, an answered prayer, something God had finally allowed after so much uncertainty. But that season did not unfold the way I expected. I lost the pregnancy at about ten weeks.

That loss broke something in me.

I became angry. I became distant. I did not want to hear about prayer. I did not want encouragement. I did not want spiritual explanations. I felt hurt, confused, and disappointed. I resented God for allowing me to experience something so meaningful only to take it away. It felt unfair. It felt cruel. It felt unnecessary.

For a while, I carried that resentment quietly.

Looking back now, I can also see how my mindset during that time was affected by pain from other areas of my life. I was dealing with emotional wounds from relationships, disappointment, and feeling unsupported. Instead of protecting what God had given me, I allowed my emotions to shape my attitude toward it. I said things out of frustration that I did not truly mean. I treated something sacred too casually. It took time for me to understand that lesson.

Not as punishment.

As growth.

Sometimes God allows us to see how we handle blessings before He entrusts us with more. Sometimes He shows us where healing is still needed. Sometimes He reveals areas where we are reacting from hurt instead of from faith.

That realization was humbling.

Trusting God again meant acknowledging that I had allowed pain from people to affect my relationship with Him. It meant accepting responsibility for my emotional responses. It meant learning how to separate disappointment from devotion.

That was not the only season that challenged my faith.

Over the years, I experienced loss on multiple levels. Losing my parents. Losing my cousin. Losing stability. Losing homes. Losing relationships. Losing seasons of life that I thought would last longer. Some of those losses were beyond my control. Others were connected to my own decisions, poor planning, and unhealthy patterns.

I had to learn how to be honest about that too.

There were times when I lost things because I did not manage them well. Times when I avoided responsibility. Times when I made emotional choices instead of wise ones. Times when I ignored warning signs. And when consequences came, it would have been easy to blame God.

But I couldn't.

Because I knew better.

Growth requires ownership.

Being homeless for the last few years was one of the biggest teachers in my life. It stripped away comfort, pride, and excuses. It forced me to examine my habits, my mindset, my discipline, and my faith. This time, I did not become angry with God. I did not feel abandoned. I understood the process. I recognized the lessons. I stayed connected spiritually even when life was uncomfortable.

That was evidence of growth.

I had reached a place where I no longer saw hardship as punishment. I saw it as preparation.

Even with the loss of my parents and my cousin, and my friend, Twin, I questioned God. I wondered why. I wrestled with grief. I felt confused. But I never disconnected. I stayed in relationship with Him, even when I did not have answers. That mattered.

Trusting God again did not mean pretending things did not hurt. It meant learning how to remain faithful while healing. It meant learning how to believe in God's goodness without needing everything to make sense immediately.

Over time, I began to see a pattern in my life. Every season that challenged my trust also strengthened my discernment. Every loss sharpened my wisdom. Every disappointment deepened my faith. Every setback refined my character.

Trust became less emotional and more grounded.

Less reactive.
More intentional.

I stopped trusting God only for outcomes and started trusting Him for direction. I stopped expecting Him to remove every difficulty and started asking Him to shape me through it. I stopped viewing faith as protection from pain and started seeing it as strength within pain.

That shift changed everything.

Today, my trust in God is not based on perfection. It is based on experience. It is built on what I have survived, learned, owned, and grown from. It is rooted in relationship, not convenience.

I trust Him because I know His voice.
I trust Him because I know His timing.
I trust Him because I know His character.

And I trust Him because I know my own now.

Trusting God again is not about returning to who you were before disappointment. It is about becoming wiser, stronger, and more aligned than you were before.

And that kind of faith lasts.

21.

Healing in Private

There is a season in personal growth when you stop explaining yourself. You no longer feel the need to give detailed updates about where you are emotionally, spiritually, or mentally. You are not trying to be mysterious. You are not trying to be distant. You have simply reached a point where your healing no longer needs an audience.

Earlier in life, many of us believe that progress should be visible. We think people should see our growth, understand our changes, and recognize our effort. We want our decisions to make sense to others. We want our boundaries to be understood. We want our distance to be respected. Over time, we realize that this expectation creates unnecessary pressure.

Not everyone will understand your process.

Not everyone needs to.

Healing in private means releasing the need for approval. It means allowing yourself to grow without constantly checking how others perceive it. It means accepting that some people will be confused by your changes and choosing peace anyway. It means being comfortable with being misunderstood while you become healthier.

I had to learn how to do that.

There were times when I wanted people to know how much work I was doing internally. I wanted them to see the effort it took to change patterns, rebuild trust, and manage emotions differently. I wanted acknowledgment. I wanted validation. I wanted reassurance that my growth was noticeable.

Eventually, I realized that seeking recognition was slowing my progress.

When you heal privately, your focus shifts inward. You become more attentive to your own behavior, mindset, and reactions. You stop measuring success by external feedback and start evaluating it by internal consistency. You ask yourself whether you are calmer, clearer, more grounded, and more disciplined than you were before.

That becomes the real measure.

Private healing also teaches restraint. You learn when to speak and when to remain silent. You learn how to protect sensitive areas of your life from unnecessary commentary. You become selective with personal information, not out of fear, but out of wisdom. You understand that some parts of your journey are too valuable to expose prematurely.

There is also freedom in not performing healing.

You do not have to prove that you are okay.
You do not have to demonstrate maturity.
You do not have to justify your boundaries.

You simply live them.

That quiet confidence changes how you carry yourself. You become less defensive and more secure. You become less reactive and more intentional. You stop engaging in conversations that no longer serve your growth.

Healing in private allows you to rebuild at your own pace. There is no pressure to rush forgiveness, accelerate trust, or skip emotional steps. You can process fully instead of partially. You can reflect deeply instead of superficially. You can grow authentically instead of cosmetically.

Over time, people notice the difference without you announcing it.

They see it in your decisions.
They see it in your boundaries.
They see it in your peace.

But by then, their opinions no longer carry the same weight.

Looking back now, I am grateful for the seasons when I stopped explaining myself and focused on becoming healthier. Those were the seasons when my growth became stable instead of temporary. They taught me how to trust my process and honor my timing.

Healing in private is not secrecy.

It is self-respect.

It is choosing depth over display.
It is choosing wholeness over attention.
It is choosing long-term peace over short-term validation.

PART 4: BECOMING

22.

Learning to Breathe Again

There is a moment in life when you realize you are no longer living in emergency mode. You are no longer waking up immediately thinking about problems that need to be solved. You are no longer constantly preparing for the next disappointment. You are no longer bracing yourself for something to go wrong. Instead, there is space in your thoughts. There is calm in your decisions. There is ease in your routine.

That moment feels unfamiliar at first.

When you have lived in survival mode for a long time, peace feels strange. Stability feels uncertain. Calm feels temporary. You almost expect it to be interrupted. You find yourself waiting for the other shoe to drop, even when nothing is wrong. That reaction is not weakness. It is conditioning.

Many of us learned how to function in chaos before we learned how to live in peace.

We learned how to problem-solve quickly. We learned how to adapt constantly. We learned how to stay alert. We learned how to manage stress. Those skills helped us survive difficult seasons.

But they also trained our minds and bodies to stay on edge long after danger had passed.

Learning to breathe again means retraining yourself to feel safe in stability.

It means allowing quiet moments to exist without filling them with worry. It means enjoying good days without waiting for bad news. It means trusting consistency instead of questioning it. It means believing that things can be calm without being fragile.

For me, this was one of the most unexpected parts of growth.

I did not realize how much tension I had been carrying until it was gone. I noticed it in small ways. I slept better. I laughed more easily. I made decisions without second-guessing myself. I stopped rehearsing worst-case scenarios in my mind. I stopped feeling responsible for managing everything at once.

Those changes were subtle, but significant.

Breathing again also meant learning how to experience joy without guilt. When you are used to struggle, happiness can feel undeserved. You may feel uncomfortable enjoying life when others are hurting or when you remember past hardships.

You may feel pressure to remain serious, cautious, or reserved.

But joy is not disrespectful to your past.

It is evidence that you survived it.

Allowing yourself to breathe again means giving yourself permission to live fully. To enjoy relationships. To pursue dreams. To laugh freely. To rest peacefully. To hope boldly. It means releasing the belief that life must always be difficult to be meaningful.

There is also spiritual growth in this season.

You begin trusting God not only in crisis, but in calm. You learn how to pray from gratitude instead of desperation. You develop consistency without fear. You walk with confidence instead of anxiety. Your faith becomes stable rather than reactive.

Over time, this way of living becomes natural.

You stop scanning for danger.
You stop expecting loss.
You stop preparing for collapse.

You start living.

Looking back now, I see that learning to breathe again was not about slowing down. It was about feeling safe in my own life. It was about trusting the stability God was building. It was about accepting peace without suspicion.

And that may be one of the greatest forms of healing.

23.

Rediscovering Joy

Joy does not always return the way you expect it to. After long seasons of responsibility, loss, and emotional endurance, many people assume that happiness will come back suddenly, like a dramatic breakthrough. In reality, joy often reenters your life quietly. It shows up in small moments, simple pleasures, and unexpected laughter. At first, you may not even recognize it.

When you have lived through difficult seasons, joy can feel unfamiliar. You become accustomed to managing stress, solving problems, and staying alert. You learn how to stay focused on what needs to be done. Over time, that mindset becomes normal. Even when circumstances improve, you may struggle to relax emotionally. You are used to being serious. You are used to being cautious. You are used to preparing for what could go wrong.

I had to learn how to release that posture.

Rediscovering joy required me to give myself permission to enjoy life again. It meant allowing myself to laugh without feeling irresponsible. It meant celebrating progress without minimizing it. It meant appreciating peace instead of questioning it. It meant recognizing that happiness was not something I had to earn through suffering.

For a long time, I associated joy with risk. If things felt too good, I assumed something bad might follow. If I felt content, I wondered how long it would last. That mindset kept me guarded. It prevented me from being fully present in positive moments.

Many people carry that pattern without realizing it.

They hesitate to celebrate.
They downplay success.
They dismiss compliments.
They rush past good moments.

Not because they are ungrateful, but because they are protecting themselves from disappointment.

Over time, I realized that withholding joy did not protect me. It only limited me. It kept me emotionally distant from experiences that were meant to nourish me. It kept me from fully receiving what God was allowing me to enjoy.

Rediscovering joy also meant reconnecting with parts of myself that had been neglected. I began paying attention to what genuinely made me smile. I noticed what energized me. I returned to activities, conversations, and environments that felt life-giving instead of draining. I became more intentional about creating space for fun, creativity, and rest.

Joy became a practice.

Not something I waited for, but something I cultivated.

I also learned that joy and responsibility can coexist. You do not have to abandon discipline to enjoy life. You do not have to ignore purpose to experience pleasure. You can be focused and fulfilled at the same time. You can be committed and content. You can be productive and peaceful.

That balance changed how I lived.

As I allowed joy back into my life, my relationships became lighter. My perspective became healthier. My confidence became more natural. I stopped seeing happiness as temporary and started viewing it as part of God's design for my life.

Looking back now, I understand that rediscovering joy was part of my healing. It was evidence that I had moved beyond survival. It showed that I was no longer defined by struggle. It reminded me that life was meant to be enjoyed, not just endured.

Joy is not shallow.

It is strength.

It is resilience.

It is restoration.

And learning how to embrace it again is part of becoming whole.

24.

When Peace Felt Possible

Let me tell you something. There comes a point in life when peace stops feeling like something people talk about and starts feeling like something you might be able to experience. Not perfectly. Not all the time. But consistently enough that you notice the difference.

And when that moment comes, it surprises you.

Because for so long, life has been loud. Busy. Demanding. Emotionally draining. You've been used to handling things, fixing things, adjusting, and pushing through. You've learned how to function under pressure. You've learned how to stay composed. You've learned how to survive.

Peace wasn't something you expected.

It felt unrealistic.

It felt like something other people had.

But then, little by little, things start shifting.

You don't react the same way anymore.
You don't panic as fast.
You don't feel responsible for everything.
You don't carry every problem like it's yours.

You start pausing before you respond. You start choosing your battles. You start protecting your energy. You start trusting yourself more.

And one day you realize, "Wait… I'm not as stressed as I used to be."

That's peace showing up.

Not loud.
Not dramatic.

Quiet.

Peace doesn't mean life is perfect. Let's be clear about that. Bills still come. People still get on your nerves. Plans still change. Disappointments still happen. But your internal world is different. You're not falling apart every time something goes wrong. You're not spiraling. You're not overthinking everything.

You're handling things differently.

And that matters.

A lot of that comes from the work you've been doing. Learning boundaries. Learning forgiveness. Learning when to speak and when to be quiet. Learning when to let go. Learning when to walk away. Learning when to rest. Learning when to trust God and trust yourself.

All of that adds up.

Peace grows when you stop entertaining chaos. When you stop engaging unnecessary drama. When you stop explaining yourself to people who don't really listen. When you stop overextending to prove your worth.

You start choosing calm on purpose.

And yes, at first it feels strange.

You might even feel guilty for being okay.

Like, "Why am I not stressed right now?"
"Why am I not worried?"
"Why do I feel… fine?"

Because you're used to struggle.

But hear me: peace is not something to feel bad about.

It's something you worked for.

It's something you prayed for.
Something you grew into.
Something you protected.

As peace becomes more normal, you notice changes in your relationships. You communicate better. You argue less. You listen more. You stop reacting emotionally to everything. You become more patient with others and with yourself.

You also start trusting God differently.

Not just when things are falling apart.
But when things are going well.

You learn how to thank Him in calm seasons, not just cry out in hard ones.

That's growth.

When peace feels possible, life feels lighter. You move with intention. You think more clearly. You sleep better. You laugh more. You feel more present.

You're not surviving anymore.

You're living.

And that's what becoming looks like.

25.

Walking in Freedom

Freedom is not something you announce. It is something you practice. It shows up in how you think, how you respond, how you choose, and how you carry yourself. Many people talk about wanting freedom, but few understand what it requires to live in it consistently.

For a long time, I thought freedom meant being free from problems. I thought it meant having fewer responsibilities, fewer obstacles, and fewer emotional struggles. Over time, I learned that real freedom has very little to do with circumstances. It has everything to do with mindset, boundaries, and self-respect.

Walking in freedom means you are no longer controlled by old patterns.

You are not making decisions out of fear.
You are not staying in situations out of obligation.
You are not shrinking to keep others comfortable.
You are not carrying guilt that no longer belongs to you.

You start choosing differently.

You choose peace over chaos.
You choose clarity over confusion.
You choose growth over comfort.
You choose honesty over avoidance.

That does not mean life becomes easy. It means you become stronger.

One of the biggest signs of freedom is emotional independence. You are no longer dependent on other people's approval to feel secure. You are no longer shaken by every opinion. You are no longer constantly questioning yourself. You trust your discernment. You trust your decisions. You trust the work you have done.

That kind of confidence is quiet.

It does not need validation.

Freedom also shows up in how you handle relationships. You love without losing yourself. You give without overextending. You listen without absorbing. You support without enabling. You communicate without attacking. You walk away when necessary without feeling guilty.

That balance takes maturity.

Walking in freedom also means taking responsibility for your life. You stop blaming your past. You stop using old wounds as excuses. You stop waiting for perfect conditions. You take ownership of your healing, your growth, and your future.

That ownership is empowering.

Spiritually, freedom means trusting God enough to live boldly. It means believing that He is guiding your steps. It means releasing anxiety about outcomes. It means moving forward with faith instead of fear.

Over time, freedom becomes your default.

You no longer overthink every decision.
You no longer replay old conversations.
You no longer carry emotional baggage everywhere you go.

You travel lighter.

You live clearer.

You love healthier.

Looking back, many people realize that freedom was not something they found. It was something they built through discipline, self-awareness, and obedience.

And once you learn how to walk in it, you protect it.

Because freedom is too valuable to lose.

26.

Living Without Apology

Somewhere along the way, many of us learned how to explain ourselves too much.

We explain why we're tired.
Why we're busy.
Why we made a certain choice.
Why we changed our mind.
Why we said no.
Why we didn't show up.
Why we moved differently.

We give background.
We give context.
We give disclaimers.

Not because we owe anyone an explanation, but because we're uncomfortable being misunderstood.

So we try to control the narrative.

We want people to know our intentions.
We want them to see our heart.
We want them to understand our reasons.

Well, you know… sometimes they won't.

And that has to be okay.

Living without apology is not about being hard. It's about being secure. It's about realizing that you do not need approval for every decision you make. You do not need validation for every boundary you set. You do not need agreement in order to move forward.

At some point, you have to trust yourself.

Trust that you thought it through.
Trust that you prayed about it.
Trust that you considered the impact.
Trust that you acted with integrity.

And then stand on it.

A lot of emotional exhaustion comes from trying to manage how people feel about your choices. You replay conversations. You worry about reactions. You draft explanations in your head. You soften your truth, so it sounds more acceptable.

That takes energy.

And over time, it drains you.

I had to learn that peace doesn't come from being understood by everyone. It comes from being honest with yourself. From knowing that you did what you believed was right, even if others didn't agree.

That shift changes how you live.

You stop over-sharing.
You stop over-explaining.
You stop defending every move.

You become quieter.
More grounded.
More decisive.

Not distant.
Not cold.

But, Centered.

Spiritually, this reflects trust. Trust that God is guiding your steps. Trust that you do not need to convince people when you are walking in alignment. Trust that obedience matters more than popularity.

Living without apology means you release the pressure to perform for people. You stop auditioning for acceptance. You stop proving your worth through explanations.

You live your life.

With clarity.
With intention.
With peace.

And that is freedom in its own right.

27.

Stronger, Softer, Wiser

Growth does not always look the way we imagine it will. When people talk about becoming stronger, they often picture confidence, resilience, and emotional toughness. When they talk about becoming wiser, they imagine clarity and good judgment. But very few people talk about softness as part of maturity.

And yet, real growth includes all three.

Over time, many of us become strong out of necessity. Life requires it. Responsibilities demand it. Circumstances force it. You learn how to push through, adapt, and carry on even when you are tired. That strength keeps you going. It teaches discipline. It builds endurance.

But strength alone is not enough.

Without softness, strength becomes rigidity. It turns into emotional distance. It makes people guarded. It teaches them how to survive, but not how to connect.

Softness is what keeps your heart open.

It is your ability to feel deeply without being controlled by emotions. It is your willingness to be honest about pain without being defined by it. It is your capacity to empathize without absorbing everything around you. It is learning how to care without losing yourself.

Softness requires courage.

It takes strength to remain kind after being disappointed. It takes maturity to remain compassionate after being hurt. It takes wisdom to stay emotionally available in a world that encourages detachment.

Wisdom is what ties everything together.

Wisdom comes from experience. From mistakes. From reflection. From lessons learned the hard way. It is the ability to recognize patterns, evaluate situations clearly, and respond thoughtfully. It allows you to move with discernment instead of impulse.

Wisdom teaches you when to speak and when to be silent. When to hold on and when to release. When to fight and when to rest.

Over time, these qualities begin to work together.

You become stronger in your boundaries.
Softer in your approach.
Wiser in your decisions.

You no longer feel the need to prove resilience. You do not need to display toughness. You do not need to broadcast growth. It shows in how you live. It shows in how you handle conflict. It shows in how you manage stress. It shows in how you love.

Spiritually, this balance reflects maturity in faith. You trust God without panic. You pray without desperation. You listen without resistance. You obey without resentment. Your relationship with Him becomes rooted in confidence rather than fear.

Stronger, softer, wiser is not a destination.

It is a way of being.

It is the result of healing, reflection, discipline, and faith working together. It reflects a life that has been shaped, refined, and aligned.

And when you reach this place, you realize that becoming was never about perfection.

It was about wholeness.

PART 5: PEACE

28.

Choosing Peace Daily

Let me be honest with you.

Peace does not maintain itself.

People think once they've healed, once life feels calmer, once things finally settle, peace will just stay. It won't. Not automatically. Peace requires intention. It requires awareness. It requires choices you make every single day.

Not big dramatic choices.

Small ones.

Daily ones.

The kind nobody sees.

Choosing peace looks like paying attention to what you allow into your mind. What you scroll past. What you entertain. What you replay. What you hold onto. If you constantly feed yourself chaos, comparison, negativity, and drama, peace will struggle to survive.

You have to be selective.

With conversations.
With environments.
With relationships.
With media.
With commitments.

That's not being "stuck up."
That's being wise.

Another part of choosing peace is learning when to disengage. Not every comment deserves a response. Not every misunderstanding needs a meeting. Not every conflict needs your energy. Some things resolve themselves when you stop giving them attention.

That takes maturity.

Peace also means learning how to pace yourself. You don't have to do everything today. You don't have to be everywhere. You don't have to say yes to every opportunity. Burnout is the enemy of peace. Overextension is the enemy of peace.

Rest is part of discipline.

Not laziness.
Not weakness.

Discipline.

Emotionally healthy people know when to pause.

Choosing peace also requires honesty with yourself. When something feels off, you don't ignore it. When you're tired, you acknowledge it. When you're overwhelmed, you adjust. You stop pushing yourself past healthy limits just to appear strong.

You start listening to your body and your spirit.

From a faith standpoint, choosing peace means staying connected to God consistently, not only in crisis. Prayer becomes a lifestyle, not an emergency call. Gratitude becomes normal, not occasional. Trust becomes steady, not conditional.

You learn how to check in with Him regularly.

And finally, choosing peace means protecting your inner world. You guard your thoughts. You challenge negative self-talk. You release resentment quickly. You forgive faster. You stop carrying unnecessary emotional weight.

You simplify.

Life becomes less complicated when peace becomes a priority.

Here's what I tell people all the time: peace is not passive. It is active. It is practiced. It is defended. It is maintained.

And when you commit to choosing it daily, everything else begins to align.

Your health improves.
Your relationships stabilize.
Your decisions sharpen.
Your joy increases.

Peace becomes your foundation.

Not something you visit, but something you live in.

29.

Guarding Your Spirit

Let's talk about something people don't always think about until they are already exhausted.

Your spirit gets tired before your body does.

You can still be working, still showing up, still handling your responsibilities, and yet feel drained on the inside. You may not even be able to explain it at first. You just know that something feels heavy. Something feels off. Something feels overwhelming in a way it didn't before.

That is usually a sign that you have been carrying more than you realized.

Many of us are natural listeners. We care deeply. We pay attention. We try to be supportive. We want to help. So when people talk to us, we take it in. When they struggle, we feel it. When they are stressed, we absorb it. Over time, without meaning to, we begin carrying emotional weight that does not belong to us.

And it adds up.

You start feeling tired even after resting. You feel irritated more easily. You lose patience faster. You feel mentally crowded. Your peace feels harder to access. None of that happens overnight. It happens slowly, through small moments of emotional overexposure.

Guarding your spirit means learning how to notice when something is affecting you more than it should. It means paying attention to how certain conversations leave you feeling. It means recognizing when certain environments drain you. It means being honest about when certain relationships require more energy than they give.

That awareness is not selfish. It is necessary.

Part of guarding your spirit is learning that you do not have to carry everything you are exposed to. You can listen without internalizing. You can care without absorbing. You can support without sacrificing your own stability. That balance takes practice, but it is essential for long-term emotional health.

It also means giving yourself permission to step back when you need to. Sometimes you need quiet. Sometimes you need space. Sometimes you need time alone with your thoughts and with God. That is not avoidance. That is restoration.

Spiritually, guarding your spirit is about staying grounded. When you stay connected to God through prayer, reflection, and honesty, your discernment becomes stronger. You become more sensitive to what is healthy for you and what is not. You begin recognizing sooner when something is disrupting your peace.

That guidance matters.

Another part of guarding your spirit is being truthful with yourself about your limits. You cannot be everything to everyone. You cannot solve every problem. You cannot pour endlessly without refilling. When you ignore your limits, burnout follows. When you respect them, balance develops.

When you begin protecting your inner world, your life starts to feel different. You think more clearly. You respond more calmly. You feel more centered. You are not easily pulled into chaos. You are not constantly overwhelmed.

Not because life is perfect.

Because you are intentional.

Guarding your spirit is one of the most loving things you can do for yourself. It allows you to show up whole, healthy, and present in the spaces that matter most.

30.

Becoming Whole

For a long time, many of us believe that healing means becoming someone new. We think growth requires erasing parts of our past, forgetting certain experiences, and leaving old versions of ourselves behind. We assume that once we are "better," we will no longer recognize who we used to be.

But that is not what becoming whole looks like.

Wholeness is not about pretending you never struggled. It is about learning how to live well with everything you have been through. It is about integrating your experiences instead of being defined by them. It is about understanding your story without being trapped in it.

You do not lose your past when you heal.

You learn from it.

Becoming whole means accepting that every season shaped you in some way. The painful ones taught you resilience. The confusing ones taught you discernment. The lonely ones taught you self-reliance. The joyful ones reminded you of possibility. All of it mattered. All of it contributed to who you are becoming.

When you begin to see your life this way, something shifts.

You stop feeling fragmented.

You are no longer one person at work, another in relationships, another in private. You begin showing up consistently. Your values align with your actions. Your beliefs align with your choices. Your inner life matches your outer life.

That alignment creates peace.

Wholeness also means learning how to hold both strength and vulnerability at the same time. You can be confident and still ask for help. You can be independent and still need community. You can be faithful and still have questions. You can be emotionally intelligent and still have moments of uncertainty.

None of that makes you weak.

It makes you human.

Becoming whole requires honesty. You must be willing to look at yourself without denial and without condemnation. You acknowledge your patterns. You recognize your triggers. You take responsibility for your reactions. You celebrate your progress without minimizing it.

That self-awareness is powerful.

Spiritually, wholeness reflects maturity in faith. It means trusting God with every part of your life, not just the areas you are comfortable sharing. It means bringing your doubts, fears, hopes, and dreams to Him without pretense. It means allowing Him to heal you from the inside out.

As you grow in wholeness, your relationships change. You communicate more clearly. You set healthier expectations. You love more freely. You stop seeking validation in unhealthy ways. You become more secure in who you are.

You no longer feel incomplete.

Not because life is perfect.

Because you are grounded.

Becoming whole is not a destination you reach and forget. It is a process you continue honoring. It requires ongoing reflection, discipline, and grace. Some days you will feel strong. Other days you will need rest. Both are part of wholeness.

When you embrace that truth, you stop chasing perfection and start cultivating balance.

And that is real growth.

31.

A Life Reclaimed

A Life Reclaimed**

There is a moment in healing that people do not talk about enough. It is the moment when you realize you are starting to recognize yourself again.

Not the version shaped by pressure.
Not the version formed in survival mode.
Not the version that learned how to numb, over function, or disappear.

You.

The one who laughs naturally.
The one who thinks clearly.
The one who feels grounded.
The one who trusts her instincts again.
The one who is not constantly bracing for impact.

That moment matters.

Because for a long time, many of us lose pieces of ourselves without realizing it. We adapt to situations. We adjust to environments. We compromise to keep peace. We silence parts of ourselves to stay safe. We shrink in places where we once felt free.

And slowly, we forget who we were before all of that.

Reclaiming your life is not about becoming someone new. It is about returning to yourself with more wisdom and more compassion than you had before. It is about honoring who you were, who you had to become to survive, and who you are choosing to be now.

There is grief in that process.

Grief for time lost.
Grief for choices made.
Grief for things that did not work out.
Grief for versions of yourself that never got to fully live.

But there is also gratitude.

Gratitude for growth.
Gratitude for resilience.
Gratitude for second chances.
Gratitude for clarity.

Both can exist.

A life reclaimed is quiet. It is not loud. It does not announce itself. It shows up in small ways. In how you talk to yourself. In how you make decisions. In how you treat your time. In how you protect your peace. In how you honor your values.

You stop abandoning yourself.

You stop betraying your needs.

You stop ignoring your intuition.

You start trusting the woman you are becoming.

Spiritually, this reflects restoration. It is God returning you to yourself. Not the wounded version. Not the fearful version. The grounded version. The one who knows Him. The one who knows herself. The one who walks with confidence and humility.

When you reclaim your life, you stop living from old narratives. You are no longer defined by what went wrong, what was lost, or what hurt you. You are defined by what you learned, how you healed, and how you chose to rise.

You live with presence.

You live with awareness.

You live with ownership.

Not in a pressured way.

In a peaceful way.

And that is when you know your life is no longer something that happened to you.

It is something you are living on purpose.

32.

Walking in Purpose

Let me tell you something I've learned over time.

Purpose is not something you suddenly discover one day and never question again. It is something you grow into. It unfolds in layers. It becomes clearer as you heal, mature, and become more honest with yourself about who you are and what you are called to do.

For a long time, many people think purpose must look impressive. They believe it must involve a big platform, a title, public recognition, or constant productivity. They assume that if their life does not look extraordinary on the outside, they must be missing something.

That belief causes unnecessary pressure.

Walking in purpose is not about chasing a spotlight. It is about living in alignment. It is about waking up each day and choosing to live with integrity, intention, and faith. It is about using what you have, where you are, to make a meaningful difference.

Sometimes purpose looks like leadership.
Sometimes it looks like service.

Sometimes it looks like building quietly.
Sometimes it looks like supporting others.
Sometimes it looks like healing yourself.

All of it matters.

One thing I often tell people is this: your purpose will always be connected to your story. The things you have survived, learned, and overcome are not random. They shape your perspective. They sharpen your compassion. They strengthen your voice. They prepare you to help others in ways only you can.

That does not mean everything you went through was fair. It means it was not wasted.

I had to learn that myself.

There were seasons when I questioned my direction. Times when I felt delayed. Moments when I wondered if I had missed opportunities or made too many mistakes. Over time, I realized that God was still working, even in the pauses. He was still preparing me, even when things felt uncertain.

Purpose is patient.

It does not rush you.
It does not shame you.
It does not abandon you.

It grows as you grow.

Walking in purpose also requires honesty. You must be willing to admit when something no longer fits. When a season has ended. When a direction needs to change. Staying stuck out of fear is not faith. It is avoidance.

Sometimes obedience looks like letting go.

Sometimes it looks like starting over.

Sometimes it looks like trusting God enough to try again.

Purpose also requires discipline. You cannot walk in what God has called you to while ignoring your health, your healing, or your responsibilities. You must care for yourself. You must protect your peace. You must stay spiritually grounded. Purpose flourishes in healthy environments.

As you continue forward, remember this: you do not have to have everything figured out to walk in purpose. You just must stay willing, faithful, and honest. You must stay open to learning. Open to correction. Open to growth.

And most importantly, open to God's leading.

Walking in purpose is not about being perfect.

It is about being present.

It is about showing up as your authentic self, trusting that God is guiding your steps, and believing that your life has meaning beyond what you can currently see.

You have done the work.

You have faced the weight.
You have released the burdens.
You have reclaimed your peace.
You have become stronger, softer, and wiser.

Now you walk forward with clarity.

With confidence.

With faith.

And with purpose.

Epilogue

Still Becoming

If there is one thing I have learned through this journey, it is this: growth does not end. Healing does not reach a final destination. Peace is not something you arrive at and never have to work for again. Life continues to unfold, and so do you.

Even now, I am still becoming.

I am still learning how to listen to myself more honestly. I am still learning how to rest without guilt. I am still learning how to trust God in new seasons. I am still learning how to release what no longer fits and embrace what is ahead. None of that makes me unstable. It makes me human.

For a long time, I believed that maturity meant having everything figured out. I thought wisdom looked like certainty. I thought strength meant never feeling unsure. Over time, I realized that real maturity is being willing to grow without pretending you have arrived.

There are still days when I reflect. Still days when I question. Still days when I adjust. Still days when I pray for clarity. Still days when I must remind myself of everything I have learned.

And that is okay.

Becoming is not a straight line. Some seasons feel confident. Others feel uncertain. Some feel peaceful. Others feel stretching. But every season carries purpose when you remain honest, faithful, and intentional.

If you are reading this and wondering whether you are "doing enough," "healed enough," or "strong enough," let me tell you this: you are exactly where you are supposed to be right now. Growth happens in layers. God works in stages. You are not behind.

You are progressing.

Still becoming means giving yourself grace. It means allowing space for mistakes, learning, and growth. It means choosing curiosity over condemnation. It means trusting that God is patient with your process, even when you are not.

It also means staying committed to your peace, your purpose, and your integrity. It means continuing to choose health over chaos, truth over comfort, and faith over fear. It means remembering that every season requires a different version of you.

And you are capable of becoming HER. Capable of becoming HIM.

As this chapter of your journey closes, another one begins. Not with pressure. Not with fear. With hope. With clarity. With confidence. With trust.

You are not finished.

You are still becoming.

And that is a beautiful place to be.

Acknowledgments

This book would not exist without the people who have supported me, prayed for me, encouraged me, and believed in me through every season of this journey.

First, I give all honor and thanks to God. For His grace, His patience, His protection, and His constant presence in my life. For carrying me when I could not carry myself. For guiding me even when I did not understand the path. For never giving up on me, even in moments when I struggled to trust Him.

To my family, thank you for being my foundation. For your love, your sacrifices, your prayers, and your unwavering support. You have been my strength in ways you may never fully realize. Everything I do is rooted in the legacy you have given me.

To my daughter, thank you for being my greatest motivation and my deepest joy. You inspire me to grow, to heal, and to lead with integrity. Watching you become the young woman you are today reminds me daily why this work matters.

To my associates, mentors, and chosen family, thank you for walking with me through every season. For listening without judgment. For speaking truth with love. For celebrating my wins and holding me steady through challenges. Your presence in my life has been a gift.

To my parents, who are no longer here in the physical sense but remain forever present in my heart, thank you. My mother once told me she was proud of me, and those words have stayed with me through every season of my life since that day. They have encouraged me when I felt unsure, strengthened me when I felt tired, and reminded me of who I am when I felt lost. I carry their love, their lessons, and their legacy with me in everything I do. This book is part of that legacy.

To every reader who picked up this book, thank you. Thank you for trusting me with your time, your heart, and your story. My prayer is that these pages remind you that you are seen, valued, and never alone in your journey. If even one chapter helped you breathe easier, think clearer, or feel stronger, then this work has fulfilled its purpose.

And finally, to myself, the younger me and the present me, I acknowledge the courage it took to write this book. To be honest. To be vulnerable. To reflect. To heal. To grow publicly and privately. This project required discipline, faith, and resilience. I am proud of the woman who committed to finishing what she started.

This book is a testimony of grace, growth, and becoming.

And the journey continues.

About The Author

Khalilah H. Purnell is an author, aspiring life coach, filmmaker, and creative entrepreneur dedicated to creating meaningful work that inspires healing, growth, and self-reflection. Through her writing and creative projects, she focuses on empowering individuals to rise above adversity and walk confidently in purpose.

With more than twenty published books to her credit, Khalilah is known for her honest, faith-rooted, and emotionally grounded approach to storytelling. Her work blends personal experience, spiritual insight, and practical wisdom to create content that is both relatable and impactful.

She is the founder of KayP Unscripted Productions and has successfully produced and released her debut feature film, *The Silent Crisis*. She is currently preparing to film her second feature project in Spring 2026, continuing her commitment to telling socially relevant and transformative stories.

As an aspiring life coach and mentor, Khalilah is passionate about helping others navigate life with clarity, resilience, and purpose. Her work reflects her belief that healing and growth are lifelong journeys that require honesty, discipline, and faith.

Peace Over Burdens represents both her personal journey and her ongoing mission to create safe spaces for reflection, restoration, and renewal. Through her writing, she encourages readers to embrace their process and walk boldly into their next season.

Khalilah continues to serve her community through creative leadership, mentorship, and faith-based initiatives. She remains committed to building legacy-driven platforms that uplift, educate, and empower future generations.

Contact Information

For updates, inspiration, and behind-the-scenes content, follow Khalilah on Instagram: **@iamkaypurnell**

Book Orders

Khalilah's books are available worldwide through all major online platforms and retailers, including Barnes & Noble, Amazon, Books-a-Million, Walmart, and other global distributors.

For bulk orders, special requests, or direct inquiries, please contact: **khalilahpurnell012@gmail.com**

Author Bookings & Appearances

To book Khalilah for speaking engagements, book signings, author visits, workshops, or special events, please contact: **bookingkhalilahpurnell@gmail.com**

Additional Works

Readers can find Khalilah's full collection of books online through major retailers and digital platforms worldwide.

Thank you for your continued support.